Oh hear ye
These simpering verses
Of suburban sensibility,
This vile creature,
A perverted poet
Peppering the page
With poisonous intent
And a fey
Wave of the wrist as if
Tossing off
Yet another sordid poem
Like it means nothing.

This vile creature,
A loathsome lurker in
Life's margins,
Ladies and gentlemen,
My name
Is Robert Garnham.

Zebra is delightfully fabulous, defiantly flamboyant, deliciously pun-packed, and definitely better than *Star Wars Episode I: The Phantom Menace*. Deep, dynamic and endearing, full of warmth and wonder. Amidst all the challenges and tough times, there is magic in this world, and Robert Garnham shows us where to find it.'

DOMINIC BERRY

'What I love most about Robert Garnham is that he seems naïve and childish enough to believe that poetry can be for the actual pleasure of the reader. His work is an invitation to spend time in his world. He's an excellent poet with an inimitable voice and a nice smile.'

MATT HARVEY

'Robert Garnham is a larger-than-life, spectacular, scene-stealing tornado of a performer. He can say serious things more seriously through apparently absurd and whimsical verse than most po-faced "intellectual" poets can through "serious" poetry. A joy to watch.'

MELANIE BRANTON

Zebra

Robert Garnham

Burning Eye

BurningEyeBooks
Never Knowingly
Mainstream

This edition published by Burning Eye Books 2017

www.burningeye.co.uk

@burningeyebooks

Burning Eye Books
15 West Hill, Portishead, BS20 6LG

ISBN 978-1-911570-16-5

Zebra

*For Mark Tunkin, Anne Hammett, Damian Rao,
Melanie Branton, and also Margoh Channing
and Dandy Darkly*

CONTENTS

THE DOORS

For those who are the exquisite hidden in cupboards.
For those who fortune denies because they refuse to shout.
For those who would otherwise shine so bright were it not so
    dark and needlessly so.
For those who are more conscious than the jaded so-called
    moral imperative.
For those who multicolour the beige.
For those who feel that burning pounding quick-tempo
    heartbeat tick-tick-ticking absolute proof down deep within.
For those who don't want to upset anyone.
For those who are being true to themselves.
For those who love.
For those who would dearly like to love but never will so long
    as they're fumbling in the pitch dark.
For those who would spread compassion if given the chance.
For those who stand tall and proud in the face of ignorance.
For those who challenge the invented with the blinding torch of
    truth.
For those who caress and whisper sweet nothings and then
    open their eyes to find an empty bed.

For those who don't want to shock and close the door voluntarily.
For those who care too much.
For those who feel they have no brothers or sisters.
For those who feel they are the only person ever ever ever ever
    to feel this way.
For those who make a thousand tiny differences a year.
For those whose revolution will knowingly take longer than their
    own lifetimes.
For those who would otherwise be flogged or hanged or
    stoned or cast from the safety of decent thought by those
    who profess to know the truth of words written fluently yet
    deliberately twisted ambiguous in order to hide the cultural
    anger seething beneath.
For those who delete their browsing history.
For those who try to prise open a door knowing that it will be
    slammed shut but keep on trying nonetheless.

For those who paid the ultimate price.

For those who resort to secret languages and those who give in and try to decipher filled with the eager promise of just knowing.

For those who are afraid.

For those who never will.

For those who see the world quivering ecstatic and reach out with trembling fingertips ever so eager to be a part yet knowing deep down they never will because they are really not as brave or as fortunate as those who colour the world with love.

For those who hide behind masks of dubious preferences just to make it look like they are one of the crowd.

For those who are furious.

For those who are curious.

For those who log on with an alias.

For those who dance ecstatic the most writhing sexual beautiful hypnotic dance but only to themselves alone alone alone in the mirror.

For those who feel that everything is hopeless faced with ninety-six percent against, newspaper editorials, fuming spitting evangelists, political bullies, idiots with guns and clubs and religious texts, charismatic spirituality, cultural commentators and peddlers of hatred.

For those who burst out so fast that the world never could catch them.

For those who burned up too soon.

For those who took a chance and flowered briefly, then disappeared, leaving behind them the hint that if done differently it might actually work.

For those who are vehement in their love.

For those who are just plain unlucky.

For those who are scared.

For those who are scarred.

For those who would otherwise be sacred.

You are the real
And your time will come
When superstition loses and common sense takes over.
Pile up your love right now
So that when the doors finally open
It will all come tumbling through.

THE STRAIGHT PUB

You've heard rumours of their existence.
Bars, pubs,
But just for straight people,
Which is kind of weird because
You don't think they'd have it in them.
I mean,
The capacity for enjoyment.
Have you seen these people?
Have you seen how miserable they look?

And you go in the door.
The thick smog of
Alcohol, sweat, disappointment,
Anti-fungal medication.
Beef-flavoured crisps,
Haynes car manuals.
It really is a straight pub.

Trying not to make eye contact.
The traditional straight greeting is
Asking what football team you support.
You've rehearsed the answer so many times.
'I like them all, they're as good as each other.'
You can't go wrong with that
In a straight pub.

Trying to act a bit more masculine.
A blokey shoulder-barge walk
Through these haggard alpha males,
Progress halted when your feet stick to the carpet.
After all, it's a straight pub.

All those ashen faces.
All those flabby cheeks.
All that denim.
Baggy misshapen jeans
On baggy misshapen men,

Curly-haired Clarkson wannabes,
The sweaters and the belchers,
The pungent and the loud,
Serial guffers and trackie-bottom Lotharios
Nursing pints as if all of life's
Frustrations can be cured by Carlsberg
And the man at the bar with the mullet,
Blank eyes staring as if in mourning
For a long-lost youthfulness.
Oh, the meaninglessness of existence!
It's a straight pub.

There's no glitter ball.
There's no dancing stage.
There's no dry ice.
The condom machine has rusted up.
As if to reinforce the status quo,
The jukebox only plays Status Quo
And someone's left a power drill on charge
By the skirting board.
It's a straight pub.

Lowering your voice an octave,
That matey blokey deep-throated straight
Thing that straight blokes have when
They talk about snooker and souped-up Subarus,
Barbecues and Sky Sports News,
Council tax and iPad apps,
Anoraks and bacon baps.
It's a straight pub.

There's a porcelain vase on the
Window sill.
It's filled with chisels.

Ordering wine – no, lager.
The barman asks which one, you say

Any, they all taste the same.
The barman says, 'I'll surprise you.'
You say, 'Oooooooh!'
The barman says, 'Pardon?'
You say, 'Oooooalll day long
I've been waiting for that!'
Good save!

Looks like you've got away with it.
Nobody suspects.
Leaning near the pool table
In a nonchalant manner,
Taking a sip of the lager and
Grimacing with the taste of it,
Accidentally sticking out your
Little finger.
Dodgy Dan looks over from the dart board,
Suspiciously.

FIRESIDE

Anger seething fake righteousness.
Visible running for miles on the prairie,
You effect some kind of masculine escape,
Topography hiding nothing.

The subtle nature of life
Provides weight where there
Never is.
But we've all convinced ourselves
Of it, breath evaporating in
The early morning mist, spirits
Of ghosts from the night before.

Cruelty cannot be undone,
Repetition of violence, stupidity
No excuse, can you hear
That rumbling sound?
Pounding across the flat terrain,
Churning up the fields,
Clods of earth flying behind
Dark horses.
Can you hear it, echoing under
Skies darkening,
A solitary scarecrow with broken bones
And a shudder, then a moan,
Then a gigantic burst of light?
Can you hear it,
Ducking for shockwaves
Flattening prairie corn?

Two thousand miles east
Eyes open with a blink
On a sultry hot radiator night.
Heartbeat increasing
Palpitations
And the sweat which comes
Through twenty years of silent craving.

BADMINTON

Two complete amateurs,
Not exactly there for the competition,
Intent only on fun,
A modicum of sporting pride,
The promise of a burger
In the pub over the road,
Having a laugh in the
Provincial leisure centre.

I must admit I'm winning,
Beating him as I invariably do,
Being such a sleek and agile sportsman,
Muscly, well proportioned,
The badminton bat an extension of my
Actual psychology.
You couldn't get anything past me.

We don't take it seriously,
Like the time, accidentally buying
Different strength shuttlecocks,
Watching them sail over the other three courts.
Whoops.
Only once, our first game,
He sat in the changing room afterwards,
A towel over my head as he uttered
Just the two words.
Well played.

I serve. He misses. We laugh.
I serve. He misses. I laugh.
I serve. He misses.
His racquet whips the air,
Hits at nothingness.
I serve. He hits it.
Whacks me in the face.
He laughs.

He serves. I hit it. He misses.
And so it goes on. I'm like a
Badminton gazelle, my muscly well-toned legs
Able to counter any attack.
He serves. I whack that mother.
Ooof, right in the goolies.

Deep in the game, now.
I am about to serve,
He lifts up his T-shirt, wobbles his
Spherical beer belly, shouts,
Wa-haaaay!
Mesmerising, his stomach gyrates and convulses
Like a crocodile trying to upchuck a half-digested zebra.
It completely puts me off my serve,
And as a scream rings out from the next court,
He laughs and I go to serve again.

She runs across our court.
That's put you off again, hasn't it? he says.
We both laugh and I try a third time,
But something isn't right.
A man, on the court adjacent,
Is on the floor.

He's hit the deck, stone cold dead.
I run over, as do others.
He lets out a groaning grasping breath.
Someone from another court begins CPR,
While I run back, phone for an ambulance,
Fingers fumbling in the jacket I'd
Slung over the net post,
As if subconsciously anticipating this.
The first aider arrives.

We can't stay here, I whisper.
I push the net post,

Then we go and sit in the changing room
Where we might philosophise,
Wonder if it's the way he would have wanted
To go,
If badminton was all he lived for,
Trying not to think of
His family.

You never know when life
Might suddenly cease.
And we were having such a good time.
My face still ever so slightly stings
Where the shuttlecock hit it.
I can still hear his last breath.

Your belly, I tell my friend,
Would've been the last thing he'd seen.
He smiles.

The game is obviously a forfeit
And one changing room locker
Will remain closed for the rest of the day.

FABULOUS

I was fabulous once
But I'm not any more.
I could reach for the heights.
Now I'm down on the floor.
I was fabulous once.
I was king of the hill.
Now the fabulous people
Just make me feel ill.

I had fabulous hair
And a fabulous grin.
I was fabulous all over
And also within.
My coat was so fabulous
And so were my shoes.
I was fabulous once.
Now that's just old news.

I was fabulous once.
Why does it vex me?
I was fabulous once
And really quite sexy.
I was ever so sweet
And very charming
But just look at me now:
It's really alarming.

I see fabulous people
On Facebook and Twitter.
I was just like them once
When I was much fitter.
I was fabulous once
But life has its limits.
I was fabulous once
For about five minutes.

GOAL

And the moment you walk in,
All that polyester
Shushing up the place,
Brand sports affiliations and
Glory by association,
Wearing a baseball cap indoors.

Sitting near your sofa,
Pretending to understand the rules,
I could teach you one or two of my own,
But until then I'll sit here
And watch corner kicks.

Men do the strangest things
When they score goals.
Some men do stranger things
And there's no football involved.

You hug me tight enough
To smell Lynx Africa antiperspirant.
I spend the rest of the match
Praying for another goal,
And your star striker,
Well known for falling over
In the penalty box.
Trip.
Trip, damn you.
Trip and roll over umpteen times.
C'mon, lad, you don't know how
Desperate I am.
I need that goal more than you think.

Polyester isn't very good
At hiding certain natural male biological occurrences.
The advice to sit down and think
About football just does not work with me.
Maybe we should turn over, I suggest.

There's a documentary about Sir Isaac Newton.
What goes up,
And all that.

How ferocious doth he blow
The final whistle, the ref.
'One nil,' you say. 'I'll take that.
Let's go off and get chips.'
'I'm OK,' I tell you. 'I'm all right.
Really, really, I'm OK.'

JOHNNY

Johnny, Johnny, Johnny, why have you now turned straight?
You no longer go all amorous when it's getting late.
I used to be your darling, now I'm just your mate.
Johnny, Johnny, Johnny, why have you now turned straight?

Danny, Danny, Danny, was this whole thing planned?
It's your sudden obsession with boobs that I don't understand.
We used to have such funky sex, now you just shake my hand.
Danny, Danny, Danny, was this whole thing planned?

Eric, Eric, Eric, you were the one for me.
I met you at a nightclub, you were so very free.
Now you're married with six kids and a mortgage and
You've got bags under your eyes and a look of
Soulless doom and oblivion every time I see you,
Which doesn't rhyme but it's the truth.

Matt, Matt, Matt, shall I call a cab?
The times we spent together were so very fab.
Now the only thing you want at night is a kebab
Matt, Matt, Matt, shall I call a cab?

Adam, Adam, Adam, was it something that I said?
I think of all the nights that we spent in bed.
Now you're mostly found with an angle grinder in your shed.
Adam, Adam, Adam, I don't even know what an angle grinder is.

Sexuality's not a fashion, like suddenly growing a beard.
All the blokes I've been with, it really is so weird.
It's like a part of their brain has suddenly become cleared.
Everything that made them gay has abruptly disappeared.

We would have stayed together had they not shown me the door.
My hopes and dreams of romance lie shattered on the floor.
I think I started to realise when not one of them begged for more.
Perhaps a night with me really was the final straw.

MY SEXY SHOPLIFTER

You are the sweetest and niftiest,
Most nimble-fingered thief and I love you.
Nonchalance is your bedfellow
And your permanent grimace is almost trout-like
Beneath the cloaked brim of your baseball cap.
Soft-skinned scally,
I want to be your ally.

Sneaking through the men's section,
Me and my tie and clipboard, and you
With a bulging Lidl carrier bag.
You know I'm there but you don't show it,
As you fumble with intent.
'Did he nick anything?' my supervisor asks.
I was looking, but I just
Wasn't looking.

One day I might have to do a strip search,
But until that time I close my eyes and
Just imagine it
As you make off with a designer jacket.

This morning, as ever, you stole my heart,
And a gentleman's wristwatch
And a hat
And a pair of jeans
And a glass decanter set
And Debs couldn't find her handbag.
'Who did this?' the policeman asked.
'Can you give a description?'
And even though I worship every inch of your face
And I can describe in depth the
Nuance of your features
From the tenderness of those kissable lips
To the sculptured aspect of your cheeks
As they slide like beauty entranced to the
Delicacy of your chin, I said,

'No, officer, it's a mystery.'

I dream of the day
You whisper to me,
'I just can't take any more.'

You lurk like a lurker
And you know that I know that I know
What you want and I know that you know
That I know what I want
And you get what you like because of it
And you don't smash my face in, that's the
Little scam we both got going here.

MATT'S DUVET

I see you
In that photo message you sent,
Wrapped in your duvet.
Why do they
Say that our love should be
The way they say it should be,
Heteronormativity?
I see you
Wrapped in your duvet.
It's such a blue day.

(THERE ARE NO GAY MEN ON) MARS

There are no gay men
On Mars.
No gay men and no gay bars
On Mars.
There's no gravitational polarity
And no homosexuality.
The magnetic field
Is null and void.
It's the sort of place
We tend to avoid.
But if the queer were here
Then at least there'd be
An atmosphere.

It takes eighteen months to go there.
Three hot-blooded men
Crammed in a sweaty module.
Things might be different
By the time they arrive.

THE MEN I LOVE ARE ALL STRAIGHT

The men I love are all straight.
I can never ask them on a date.
They only want to be my 'mate'.
The men I love are all straight.

It's such a strange perversion.
To me they show an aversion.
I'm secretly hoping for a conversion.
They're so annoyingly straight.

I feel so very pessimistic.
I have to work out the logistics
To get them and take risks
Or tempt them with cheese and onion crisps.

It really is so tragic.
To be with them would be magic,
But they're all so monosyllabic.
They're so annoyingly straight.

I try so hard to make passes.
Straight lads have got such great arses.
And their legs, so long and slender.
There's no way that they'll turn bender.

It's such a cruel conception.
It gives me such dejection.
I'll never get to see him with a…
Coffee first thing in the morning.
They're so annoyingly straight.

When will this madness end?
It drives me round the bend.
I plead to them, just pretend
That I'm more than just your friend.

Oh, the message to the world we could send.
We could start our own new trend.

But I just cannot comprehend
The behavioural heteronormative barriers of
False cultural conceits plus your weird
Fascination with angle grinders.

It's hard not to feel so hurt.
You repel me each time I flirt,
Then walk around without your shirt.
And your buttocks, so magnificently pert.

The men I love are all straight.
Half an hour with one would be great.
Till then I can only
Speculate.
'Cause the men I love are all straight.

POEM

The salmon
Who survives
Carries the memory
Of her lost siblings.

Born to spawn,
Born to fight currents,
Born to survive,
To perpetuate.

Hey, salmon,
Stop a while.
There's more to life
Than the
Ceaseless
Inanity of the
Generations.

And the salmon says,
'Like what?'

And then carries
On her way.
And only much later
Do I think
I should have said,
'Custard cream biscuits.'

OBLIVIOUS

I carefully worship his constituent parts,
But he's annoyingly oblivious,
As if the effect of my sad devotion
Is the true price of sharing existence,
The absolution of his being,
And of his being absolutely gorgeous:
A solid fact.

I eulogise his face and eyes,
Rhapsodise his gracefulness,
Enmeshed as he is in nonchalance
For it is his right to be so
Utterly beautiful yet emotionally undriven,
And my worship a given,
A solid fact.

Yet often I ponder that his obliviousness
Would be cheapened if, by chance,
He were to let me in.
I could never be with a man so imperfect
As to spoil perfection by breaking a spell
So wondrous.

POEM

Every day he comes, the sparrow,
To the window of Mr Pinkerton, who feeds him,
Sprinkles crumbs on the sill and watches,
Attentive, behind glass as the cock
Pecks at bread.
For some reason Mr Pinkerton calls the sparrow 'Josh',
And eulogises the beauty of nature,
Insisting that the daily ritual of feeding Josh
Fills him with an indescribable gratitude.

One day he went away, Mr Pinkerton, and he asked
That I should come round and feed the bird,
Come round at the crack of dawn and marvel
At nature in its celestial, timeless magnificence.
OK, I said,
And I fed the sparrow.

You smug tiny tweeting bastard.
You indiscriminate crumb muncher.
You pert-beaked obtrusive harbinger of pox.
You natural corruption of foul and soulless doom.
You beige-rumped teaser void of all emotion.
You flying bollocks.
You impulsive defecator on fresh-hung wash-line linen.
You tit.
You flappy wittering puke-inducer.
You chirruping obnoxious symbol of general malaise.
You insidious platform of misery.
You flitting nonsense enmeshed in tedium and sordidness.
You who reaches deep in my soul with your fluttering
    feathered limbs, wrenching from my subconscious all
    pretence of pleasure, as if the pomp of your existence
    should guarantee the continuance of your sick and putrid
    being.
You who tears all hope from the sky and blackens it with the
    cruel brush of insensitivity as if in celebration of our finite
    lives and looming mortality.

You who mocks the vanity of our own private existentialist
    justifications for continued existence.
Josh.
I don't like you very much.

The next day Mr Pinkerton came back from his trip
And I phoned, asking if Josh had
Seemed okay that morning, to which he replied that
He seemed quite chirpy.

POEM

I'd love to be a trawlerman
Floating on the sea.
Out there on the ocean,
I would be so free.
Surrounded by the briny deep,
A bunk at night is where I'd sleep.
I'd love to be a trawlerman
Floating on the sea.

Fishy fishy fishy fishy,
Fishy one two three.
Fishy fishy fishy fishy,
Out there on the sea.

I'd love to be a trawlerman.
A boat is where I'd be.
I'd love to be a trawlerman
Out there on the sea.
I'd love to be a trawlerman.
It is no disgrace.
I'd love to be a trawlerman.
At least I know my plaice.

Fishy fishy fishy fishy,
Fishy one two three.
Fishy fishy fishy fishy,
Out there on the sea.

When no one's looking I sneak down
To the fish hold in the
Belly of the ship,
Take off all my clothes and
Slither among their scaly euphoric slipperiness.

POEM

Discordant squeaking and honking
Like a modernist orchestral piece
As a gang of clowns gone bad
Runs away from the police.

POEM

Liquid fuel pressurised.
Checked the figures like a man obsessed.
Flick flick fingernail on gauge case.
Yes, looks about right, daddy-o.

Careful careful moved it on to my back,
Backpack jetpack, one final energy-
Boosting flapjack and the agony
Of the launch sequence.

Watch me watch me watch me soar watch me
Gloop and glide and swoop and slide
Dancing on clouds like a hotmetal angel
Because this is what I have been waiting for,
It's what I have always wanted, to conquer
The obvious and feel myself become sublime
As I stick two fingers up at both
Convention and gravity,
One final check of the dials and
WHOOOOOOSH!

Kapow.
Crack.
Kazoom.

Forgot to do up the straps and the
Bloody thing flew off without me.

POEM

Josh, darling
So pristine
As to be/
Cyborg

I cannot envisage
Your beauty/
Night lasers
Plastic Josh
System reboot

Upgrade necessary
Pending
Disk full

Josh, sweetness
Enmeshed in beauty/
Imminent
Failure
Your/
Error

10.1.16

What could be worse
Than a Monday morning in January
Back at work after an indifferent weekend
And Bowie being dead?

I would have danced and dreamed
Because there was nothing else
Needed doing
But the days went by too fast.

There are murmurs and science
And darkness around the most vivid light
But the rhythms which hold us
Are all man-made, and now we've got to

Go in to work and do all the usual things,
Keep busy and maintain some kind of
Professionalism, stars, black light, dancing,
Lost in music, and Bowie still dead.

POEM

There's a badger in the garden
And it thinks it's on *EastEnders*.
There's a badger in the garden
And it thinks it's on *EastEnders*.

Having arguments
With other badgers,
Arguments
With family members,
Arguments and arguments.
It thinks it's on *EastEnders*.

Hey there, badger.
What's going on?
Hey there, badger.
Whatever's wrong?
Hey there, badger,
Are you filled with ennui
And angst about life in the
Postmodern world?
Or do you think
You're on *EastEnders*?

There's a badger in the garden
And it thinks it's on *EastEnders*.
There's a badger in the garden
And it thinks it's on *EastEnders*.

And I said,
Shoo, Mr Badger,
Shoo and go away.
Shoo, Mr Badger,
Shoo and go away,
And the badger said,

You 'aving a larf or something?
What's all this abaaaaht?

POEM

I jump from concrete road bridge
On to the train roof,
Land on both feet simultaneous.

The bad guy has a shooter,
And we run,
Ducking other bridges,
Signalling equipment.
Suburban detritus.

Captured, he pins me down,
Gritted teeth,
I kick his gun away,
Knee him in the goolies
As we tumble like jelly in a
Washing machine
On the buffet car roof.

The train stops.
I have him round the neck.
The train stops.
He gives me a Chinese burn.

The train is delayed, cancelled.
Jump down to the platform,
Then on to the roof of a
Rail replacement bus,
Helped up by aid of a ladder,
Still fighting.
I give him a slapping
As we pull away,
He flicks my nose with his forefinger,
I bite his arm,
He stamps on my foot.
I hop.

And as the bus pulls out on to

The first of many rural back roads
And branch line stops, he
Resorts to tickling, and I
Call him a name, and then we
Whack each other with pillows,
And then we laugh, and just lie there
On the bus roof as the rail replacement
Service stops at some lights,
Indicating left,
Waiting for a break in the traffic.

HAIKU

The man with no arms
Fighting in the local pub.
He was kicking off.

POEM

You took me to the
Smoke Alarm Museum.
I got a bad neck
From looking up at all the
Smoke alarms.

I thought, I'll end it
When we get to the café.
Tell you how I feel.
It's not you, it's me.

A trays of teas and a sticky bun
And you showed me the novelty rubber
You'd bought
In the shape of a smoke alarm.

'I'll put it on my desk,' you said,
'Next to the other one
From the Lampshade Exhibition.
And by the way, how's your neck?'

'Easing now,' I said.

Some of the smoke alarms
Had been quite baroque
And we'd stood in a hushed silence
In the Nazi smoke alarm section
And you said your favourite
Was a smoke alarm once owned by TS Eliot.

The low evening sun
Tenderly caressed your handsome features.

'Easing now,' I repeated.

POEM

Flappy flappy flappy
And a wavy wavy wavy,
Dissipating smoke from the
Smoke detector.
Flappy flappy flappy
And a wavy wavy wavy.
Hasn't gone off yet.
Any second now it might.
Toast burned, toast burned,
Black smoke pouring out,
Lifting up into the room,
Adding to the morning gloom.
Flappy flappy flappy
And a wavy wavy wavy.
Along comes a dinosaur,
Big grumpy dinosaur,
Mistakes my mad flapping for a
Prehistoric moth
And eats me.

POEM

If love were a general,
What would that make me?
An insurgent? A rebel?
Or merely
A sandwich in his waste paper bin?

He would match on me.
He would munch on me.
He'd see in my eyes
The enemy.
He'd have a hunch.
He'd have a lunch.

Coming in after a hard day
Square bashing,
Seeing yesterday's sandwich
In the bin
With a sense of
General malaise.
It's chicken mayonnaise.

A POETRY GIG IN THE AMAZON BASIN

Thick dense jungle vegetation.
A circle of audience members in a hut by a swamp
By the banks of the mighty Amazon,
Peering at me, nervously I approach
A microphone which buzzes, or maybe it's the
Mosquitoes, wondering how I ended up here,
And whether to do my famous poem about Lidl.

Thirteen hours by plane from Heathrow, six hours
By internal flight to Manaus, seventeen hours
By pick-up truck, then a boat ride, followed by
Six hours' trek through jungle vegetation led by
A man in a hat with a machete, to this place,
A hut near a mining settlement, only to be
Greeted by puzzled frowns. There's been a
Booking mix-up. They were expecting Pam Ayres.

Preliminary chit-chat to break the ice.
'Isn't it annoying,' I tell them, 'when you're baking a
Soufflé, and it doesn't rise properly?'
'The rainy season floods took my house away,' someone
Helpfully pipes up, I decide not to perform
My new poem about temperamental vacuum cleaners.
I decide on a joke. 'I hear you have electric eels here
In these parts,' I tell them, 'I've heard about them; they
Sound shocking.' In the silence that follows I hear the
Distant hooting of parrots.

The relentless humidity causes beads of sweat
To roll down my face like the last lingering hopes
I once had that this would be a good gig,
Having taken with me through the jungle, on the back of
A mule which complained most vociferously all the way,
Twenty copies of my book titled *101 Things Not to Do
At Junction 13 of the M25*, plus the sudden realisation
They my fee of sixty quid probably wouldn't cover
The four days of travel from Basingstoke to here.

Headlining next month, apparently,
Is Kate Tempest.

Distant thunder rumbles.
Fat lazy drops fall from the sky,
Falling on fleshy leaves like polite theatre applause.
I make a final effort to tell them some half-baked
Anecdote about a wellie-throwing contest at the annual
Village fete in suburban Surrey where I grew up, only
For the audience to respond with a smattering of applause,
Possibly glad of this chance to learn about a different, strange
    culture.

The next act after me does some
Urban street dancing, and the audience loves
Every second.
It's always difficult going on first.

THE MOOR POETS

I've been hanging out with the Moor Poets.
One of them tried to show me some limestone,
And another
Eulogised a pony
And I made some wisecrack about
There not being a Starbucks near.

I've been hanging out with the Moor Poets,
All anoraks and rhyming dictionaries
And the word 'bleak' being bandied around.
And one of them tried to find a rhyme
For 'drizzle'.

I've been hanging out with the Moor Poets.
I told them that the rhythmic flap-flap
Of the pheasant's wings
As it takes to flight, gracefully,
Kind of reminds me of a nightclub,
Disco thump beat pounding life's rhythms deep,
Deep into my soul.
Oh, how majestic the flight
Of the noble pheasant
In all its pheasanty glory!

I've been hanging out with the Moor Poets
Hey, I said,
When do we get to overrun eleventh-century
Spain
And build the Alhambra?
Nobody laughed.

I've been hanging out with the Moor Poets.
Three hours in the rain on a sodding riverbank
Trying to see a sodding otter
So that we can write sodding sonnets
About sodding otters
And yet when I get out my iPad

And go on to Wikipedia,
Somehow I'm seen as the weird one.

I've been hanging out with the Moor Poets,
Pointing out that the sound the car makes
As it goes over a cattle grid
Sounds like an old lady farting on a bus.
They all made plans to meet again
Next month,
But to me they just said,
Thanks for coming.

POEM

I love whistling.
I do it when I'm feeling jaunty,
Whistling,
You could never hurt or taunt me
When I'm whistling
I put my lips together
And I give it all I've got.

I love whistling,
Shows the world that I'm contented,
Whistling,
My hopes and dreams never have been dented
When I'm whistling.
You know you cannot hide
When it comes from deep inside.

POEM

after Sylvia Plath

After you, says Sylvia Plath.
No, after you.
No, I insist, says Sylvia Plath.
Are you sure? I enquire.
No, go on, she says.
I really do insist, I tell her.
Age before beauty, says Sylvia Plath.
How's your mother? I ask.
It's raining, says Sylvia Plath.
I saw an otter today, I tell her.
Cold out here, isn't it? says Sylvia Plath.
After you.
No, after you.
Someone make up their mind,
For goodness' sake,
Says Pablo Picasso.

STATIC/WIND

Voices coming through the static.
Distant radio stations lost in time.
Eerie crackling from faraway lands.

And it's a hot summer night.
And you can't sleep.
And everything's so still it's like
The energy's building up.
Strange voices coming through the static.

And the radio signals bounce from wistful antennas.
And there's something Saharan about existence.
And you can't breathe because of all the dust
Choking the neon.
Strange voices coming through the static.

'You could be a winner
If only you had the luck.
Don't leave me, babe.
Don't leave me, babe.
Please don't give me up.'

Strange voices coming through the static.

'You were my last infatuation.
You were my last euphoria.
So, honey, you might as well
Stay stay stay with me.'

Strange voices coming through the static.
And it sounds like they're talking to me.

'You are Robert.
No one else is.
You are Robert.
Only one of you.'

I am my own history.
I am my own self.
I am my own spirit.
There is no one else.

Strange voices coming through the static.

THE INCREASING PHYSICAL DEXTERITY OF JUSTIN BIEBER

With each day that passes
The physical strength of Justin Bieber increases.
His dexterity and agile nature
Are evident in any fight situation.
If someone's acting in a menacing manner
It's him I want on my side.
He's growing up.
He's more sure of himself.
His muscles are developing
And he's learning how to use them.
Biebs is on a mission!

I'm less sure of myself.
My own puny wimpy life is riddled
With inconsequentialities.
I have neither the tenacity,
The agility, nor the mesmerising hair
Of Justin Bieber.
I do the washing up and I
Take out the recycling,
All the time
Pondering on his increasing physical strength.
Pretty soon he will devour us all!

As his body develops it begins to take on
The chiselled nature of a classical statue
And his poise evokes the work of Michelangelo.
The subtle layering of muscle on bone structure
Affords him the upper hand in any hostile scenario.

If he were any more statuesque,
He'd be a statue.

Blessed be he, oh Bieber who makes us gibber and quake.
Blessed be he with the thunder in his chest.
Blessed be he, fortune sun ray multilinear postmodernist
    zeitgeist bunny flip-flop.

Blessed be he, mighty mighty towering colossus of pop.
Blessed be he with his interesting collection of tattoos.
Blessed be he with the existentialist duplicity of living.
Blessed be the hours I've spent in contemplation of his greatness.
 Blessed be the overriding poetry of his music, oh how it grabs
     you in the heart.
Blessed be the world as it spins and it turns and it shines
All on account of his increasing physical dexterity.

He uses his fists with skill and with lightning reflexes.
You can't actually see what he's doing because
He moves quicker than light.
He excels in acrobatics like a Shaolin warrior,
Seemingly defying gravity, which serves to blind his
Enemies; see them cower in confusion!
He'd be called the Flash, or the Lightning Bolt,
If he weren't already known as Justin Bieber.
He's got a mind as pure as the Dalai Lama
And as calculating as a calculator.

Last night, a thief stole my mobile phone
And Biebs,
Like a shapeshifting berserker
Of Icelandic folklore,
Tore into the chap,
Not only returning my phone
But also belting out
One of his hit songs.
I don't know which one it was.
They all sound the same.

2 ABBEY 1

Frost-clung sun and scratchy ear-splitting aircraft
In the cold winter morning.
The thrum and hum of motorway traffic
Filtered through sliding 1980s windows,
Chalk dust swirling in a low-slung sunbeam.

Darren arrives first with his spiky hair and
Ever-present grin, all new and fresh,
Baby of the class.
Not terribly bright, he swore blind that
The current US president was Abraham Lincoln
And he couldn't understand why people in Dublin
Spoke English.

I look like a ghost,
Feeling old even then.
These kids will soon be men
And I'll never see them again.

Then the lads come in,
Fresh from a morning kickabout,
Justin, Justin, Paul and Justin,
Big-mouthed lairy lads smelling of hair products,
Diesel exhaust from suburban bus rides,
Cheap aftershave even though
None of them shave,
All with the same hairstyles modelled on
Pop music heartthrob Rick Astley
And kids' TV presenter Andy Crane.

Others filter in,
Jocks and sports aficionados,
Deep-throated spotty Jack-the-lads,
Male bimbos and the terminally odd,
Random souls thrown together by
Secondary school scheduling,
Quoting football statistics and carrying

Sports equipment emblazoned with
Various London team logos,
The air thick with teenage hormones and
Estuary accents, mock-Cockney,
Strange sudden Americanisations they've learned
From watching *The A-Team*.

They josh and joke and joke and josh,
Joking about football,
Joking about football managers,
Joking about football teams and football players
And football supporters,
And I tell them that I'd like to join in
With all this football-based jocularity
But I don't know anything about football,
So when it comes to football jokes
I'm stumped.
None of them laugh.

Next would arrive Omar,
Sensitive intellectual who, unlike me,
Would mug up on the football results the
Night before so as not to be left out.
And Alan, anonymous Alan who
Was just one of the lads,
And Phil, who in all of our four years
Never once did or said anything remotely noteworthy.
It seemed our class had ever conceivable type
Of the stale stereotypical representations,
Except that there were none of those slightly camp
Nerdy types you often see.
Though hang on a minute,
That was probably me.

Not exactly the class clown,
I was seen more as a sage, a
Prototype Alan Bennett, not least because

I'd memorised comedy one-liners,
My speciality being New York Jewish stand-up
Delivered in the poshest Surrey accent.
Even then I was pretty weird.
But it saved me from getting beaten to a pulp
Every break time.

Frequent laughter and boisterousness.
One of the Justins would break wind
And all of the other Justins would laugh as if
It was the funniest, most whimsical amusement of the decade,
And Darren and Wayne would argue because
They couldn't remember the name of the family in
Bigfoot and the Hendersons.

It was the Hendersons.

I hated these losers with a passion.

I hated Justin's hyperactive shrieking.
I hated the way Paul would belch and then
Everyone would laugh
And others would then start belching,
Getting bigger laughs than I got with one of my
Carefully constructed Neil Simon-esque one-liners.
I hated the way that Alan would copy everything
That Justin did
As if Justin was a philosopher of the age,
Even when the thing that Justin had just done was
Downright mean and vindictive.
I hated the way that the whole lot of them
Would laugh and laugh and laugh if any word
Sounded like it might rhyme with 'knob', 'bum', 'tit',
'Wank', 'anus', 'butt' or 'boob'
And yet when I'd point out that Arsenal
Started with the word 'arse'
They'd just nod blankly and say,
'Your point being?'

I hated these kids.
I hated these muppets.
Gary with his mullet.
Dan with his beef-flavoured crisps.
Wayne, who smelled like beef-flavoured crisps.
Justin with his runny nose.
Paul, who swore that wrestling was real.
I hated them all apart from Darren, whose spiky hair,
Even after all these years,
I still copy just to be like him.
I hated them, and I wanted to escape.

As I say, these kids
Became men.
I see them on Facebook now,
Old and fat and bald and married.
None of them ended up playing for Arsenal,
None of them made it as a professional wrestler,
They're now plumbers, managers,
Dads and granddads,
And that's when it strikes:
They think I'm still sitting there
In that tutor group room
And they all escaped from me.

THE PRINCE OF BELGIUM

Bored of the humdrum.
Bored of the same old.
Bored of the logic.
The history I created for myself.

Bored of the suburbs with all their suburban psyche ever so
    frightening never struck by lightning hardly ever fighting
    conservatory-clung backyard train line whistle-whip
    suburban suburban nothing.
Bored of the trains.
Bored of the quiet streets with their brown brick identical
    departmental uniformity.
Bored of the planes.
The history I created for myself.

Bored of the A30.
Bored of the M25 with its orbital four-lane crawler-lane corridor
    lights strung round at night in their sodium glare like a
    string of pearls around London's chubby neck.
Bored of Junction 13, Staines.
The history I created for myself.

Bored of my friends.
Bored of Paul.
Kevin.
Malcolm with the runny nose.
Bored of Darren with his spiky hair facial hair glacial stare
    neither here nor there and the times we spent in his small
    flat over the greengrocer's where I first
Bored of Helen.
Natasha.
Bored of all the girls.
Bored of the village green.
The history I created for myself.

Bored of London.
Bored that it should be just out of reach.

Bored of the quivering fingertips outstretched, never touching.
Bored of the airport with its terminals and taxiways and tower
    blocks and takeaways and taxi ranks and terrorists.
Bored of the planes with their jet range long haul and their
sharp fins like shark fins negotiating Hounslow hangars like the
opening scene in *Jaws*.
Bored of the history I created for myself.

Bored of the ethos.
The memories.
Bored of telling the same old story with its half-lies and
    masked lives, its allegations and feigned surprise, hints
    and suppositions and nice tries, concealments and
    congealments, corruptions of the honest in all its truth-
    stealing layer-peeling, nerve-breaking heart-rending
    action-defending comedy-dependent occasionally-
    resplendent ancestor-descendent shelf-replenishment life
    of mine in which absolutely nothing happened.

KATE

She stood before me
On a sultry summer Surrey night,
The stone steps to her parents' flat
Radiating the day's heat,
Bricks soaked with sun sweat,
Sweet dust smells and caramels
And the subtlety of Kate's fragrance,
Ever so delicate.
The moment was so beautiful.

And so was Kate.
Her cousin was a former Miss World.
Her aunt was married to a very famous
Film star.
Kate,
Californian Kate with Guyanan ancestry,
Skin so soft like coffee,
Wide cinnamon eyes filled with love on that
Exotic sin-drenched August night,
Standing before each other
In a moment of the purest romance.

Yet
I felt nothing.
Worse,
I could sense a dark chasm
Deep inside of me,
Swallowed down with every lie,
Every untruth, every evasion,
So obvious as to obliterate all but my own
Teenage fabrications,
And Kate, culturally American,
Who saw in me the mannerisms
Of a Disney gentleman
As we bent for a kiss on those
Sun-baked steps,
Gazing in each other's eyes
Like lovers are meant to.

What do you want?
I don't know what I want.
How can I reach you?
I think it's impossible.
Is it something I've done?
I think I just need a little time.
Time for what?
To get my head in order.
Why are you lying to me?
You're not the only person I'm lying to.

Her hand in mine,
Soft and small and warm,
Her cotton summer dress
Falling down to her delicate sandals
With a modesty that so many others
Found truly alluring as I
Fantasised a Hollywood wedding
And saving myself for our
First night of bliss.
An air-conditioned kiss,
Plenty of time to steel myself,
Brace for her beauty,
So brave,
So brave.

I always knew.
But I can explain.
Every time I looked at you.
Please don't do this.
We were both young. We were both stupid.
I tried to change.
It's who you are.
Please don't do this.
Why couldn't you ever tell the truth?

Because it was impossible.

Certain processes and cultural
Associations,
None of which can excuse the
Failure to ignite that which only
Half-smouldered,
Or to grasp a truth so vital
As to stay hidden potentially forever.

She stood before me
As the deep blue sky
Smudged itself brown on traffic fumes,
As we parted just with a
Peck on the cheek,
A short walk home, relieved to have endured
And prolonged the pretence
To a family happy to have their Romeo return,
And everything right with the world.

(YOU'RE JUST NOT) FLAMBOYANT

I never knew, he said.
You're not flamboyant, or anything.
In fact you look like a normal bloke.
Jeans and a T-shirt.
That's what normal blokes wear, isn't it?
Jeans and a T-shirt.
Maybe not a T-shirt which reads,
'I can't even think straight'.
I thought you were wearing it for a bet.

So we're still going to be friends, right?
You're not going to start fancying me,
Are you?
So you're still going to like
Cheeseburgers?
And action films?
You're not going to start fancying me,
Are you?
You're not going to start dancing to
Kylie, and wearing foundation,
Are you?
You're not going to start baking quiches,
Are you?
You're not going to start
Wearing scarves
And buying cushions
And calling people 'darling',
Are you?
You're not going to start fancying me,
Are you?
Are you?
You're not going to start fancying me,
Are you?
I mean, that's disgusting.

Isn't it?

I always suspected it.
I could tell by the way you nibble sausages.
I could tell by the way you fondle tangerines.
I could tell by the way you would stop talking
Whenever Adrian Chiles came on the TV.
I could tell by the way you knew instinctively
What colour lampshade to buy.
That can't be taught.
It's genetic.

I could tell by the way you would
Dance like a camp dinosaur,
Flappy-handed
Floppy-fringed camp dinosaur,
Sidestep shuffle floppy floppy
Camp camp dinosaur.
That's how I could tell.
Hello, I'd say to myself,
Hello,
What's going on here, then?
Camp camp dinosaur.

I don't know why you told me, though.
Things were fine the way they were.
It explains why you weren't so keen
On that film last week.
That excellent film.
That excellent lesbian porn film.
That excellent classic of its genre,
Hot Girls Gagging for It,
During which you did the crossword.
I couldn't understand why
You didn't like the lesbian porn film.

I understand now, though.

But I'll still be your friend,

Your buddy, your mate.
We'll still do the things
That normal lads do.
All the usual japes and hijinks,
The usual mucking around,
The usual rough and tumble,
The same old playfulness and manly
Shenanigans, the same old
Roister-doistering, the same old
Mock-serious playfighting,
Rolling and tumbling,
Hand-to-hand physical matey
Bonding that we always did,
The same old faux-serious
Slap and tickle and giggling
Like exhausted schoolgirls, floppy tired
Little puppies slumbering together
On your bed semi-naked
Because it's so hot.

Why couldn't you tell me?
You're not flamboyant, or anything.
How was I to know?

JAMIE

This is a poem about how I met Jamie.
I'd seen lots of men
But they all looked a bit samey.
Jamie was different,
His hair was bleached,
Which on others looked lamey,
But he oozed excitement; can you blame me?
He said he wanted to lay me.
Jamie,
Not big on subtlety.

He asked me out on a date.
I said, 'Wait,
I mean, really?
Have you seen me?
You don't look at my profile picture
And fear me?
Though it is about fifteen years out of date.'
He texted back,
'It's happening,
I look at you and I see true bliss,'
And he added a kiss.
It was hard to miss.
He'd done it in upper case,
Which frankly I found ostentatious.
But my appetite was voracious
And I tried to act all gracious,
Which I ruined by replying
Yes yes yes yes yes yes please,
Oh yes, definitely,
Oh yes, gosh!

We went out for a meal.
He asked if I was real,
So sly his gestures, he
Seemed afire with a burning zeal.
He said he had a hunger that was

Burning deep within.
I said me too,
I didn't have any lunch today.
He said he had certain urges
And quoted me beautiful verses
Which I took to be a Byronic romanticist
Ode to a dead poet's fiancé.
Turned out it was actually Beyoncé.

He said he wanted to take it further.
I said I was thinking of having the burger.

We went to a nightclub.
He asked me to dance.
I said no chance.
I'd probably end up
Splitting my pants.
The music was loud,
The lasers so bright,
And at 10pm
It was the latest I'd been up at night.
There wasn't a person over thirty in sight.
The room was filled with hormones
And acne.
It wasn't for me.
It wasn't to be.
I asked at the bar for a cup of tea.

But you danced, Jamie,
You danced with all your might,
A rhythmic blurry maelstrom of the night
Writhing with sexual innuendo,
Contorting your lithe T-shirted frame.
I knew that I would never be the same
As you pounded, gyrated at one with the beat,
Enmeshed with the rhythm the excitement the heat.
I could feel strange stirrings from my head to my feet

And all of a sudden I started to dance,
To lose myself to the music.
Not sure how to do it,
And not sure how it goes,
I flailed my arms and, crack!
Broke someone's nose.

Waiting on the street for a cab,
A sudden yearning for a kebab.

A backstreet taxi takes me
Amid backseat fumbles
To the gateway of maybe,
Jamie,
To your flat share, sat there,
Feebly offering a fiver to help
Pay for the cab fare,
Allergies playing up
Because of all the cat hair,
Kissing like I've never been with any other,
Not minding that we have to be quiet
So as not to wake your brother,
Not minding that you have
A Jean-Luc Picard duvet cover.

Because I like you
And I like it that I like you
And you like me and I like it that you like me
And you like it that I like you
And I like it that you like it that I like you
And you like it that I like it that you like me.
Well, isn't that just like me?
There's so much liking going on.
I also like the look of that box of doughnuts on the side,
But on the whole we like each other
Enough to start doing the things that we both like
And that is how we spend the night.

Jamie,
It wasn't to be.
The times I spent with you were bliss
And to ponder on reasons
For our break-up would be remiss,
But every text you sent
Had an upper case kiss
And for some reason
That was really annoying.

INTEGRITY

I'm me.
And I have been now
For as long as I can remember.
There were times when I tried to be
Someone other than me.
Like when I pretended to be a car.
But it always backfired.

I was so intrepid, back then!

Like when Ben said he liked
The colour magenta, walking in meadows,
And the soft downy fur of baby ducks,
And I said I liked
The colour magenta, walking in meadows,
And the soft downy fur of baby ducks,
And then he dumped me.

Like when Rhys said he liked
Petrol station neon, the smell of glossy magazines,
And the feeling of writing on a banana skin,
And I said I liked
Petrol station neon, the smell of glossy magazines,
And the feeling of writing on a banana skin,
And then he dumped me.

Like when Andrew said he liked
Dire Straits, Jeremy Clarkson
And any film starring Jason Statham
And I said
Good luck with all that.
He still dumped me.
But at least I kept my integrity.

And that made me feel
Kind of glad, in a way.

And I'm me right at this present moment.
That's what it's all about.
I've never been me more than I am
Right now.
And maybe in the future I will look back
At all this and think,
Wow,
I was really me back then!

LITTLE HOUSE

I'd like to live in a little house
Somewhere in the park.
I'd have to light lots of candles
Whenever it gets dark.
I'd buy myself a little dog
Just to hear it bark.
(Woof woof!)
And I'd invent new grammar and
A punctuation mark.

Tiddly om pom pom
Tiddly om pom pom

And as the winter splinters in
I'd have to light the fire.
I'd collect lots of ornaments
And things that I admire.
I know it's not the sort of life
To which you might aspire.
It would be just like a church
Except without a spire.
Or a monotheistic deity.

Tiddly om pom pom
Tiddly om pom pom

And I would write such poetry,
Making sure it rhymed,
And I would use a stopwatch
Just to check its pace.
It would be a fantasy
Away from the daily grind.
I would cuddle the handyman.
I'm sure he wouldn't mind.

Tiddly om pom pom
Tiddly om pom pom

And did I mention the handyman?
We'd cuddle up in bed.
Such a randy handyman
I'd keep him in the shed.
And every time I was up for it,
'Oh Fred,' I'd call, 'oh Fred,'
Although his name is actually Sean.
At least he gives good

Tiddly om pom pom
Tiddly om pom pom

It doesn't matter what we do.
Our lives are meaningless.
Nowt but crushing oblivion
And eternal hopelessness
And never-ending loneliness
And doubt and angst and hatred
And the enduring tyranny of Living,
The eternal dichotomy between selfhood
And the final and crushing truth that
No one has ever cared for you in the slightest.

Tiddly om pom pom
Tiddly om pom pom

POEM

He brandishes broccoli
Outside the station,
Waving it at commuters.
'Look at my broccoli,
Look at it!
Look!'
I hurry past, intent to avoid,
While not acting improperly,
This broccoli cacophony,
As I pass into the station,
And I admit to some hesitation as
I prepare to hear his views
On his choice of vegetation,
But instead he says,
'Robert?'

And I say,
'Mum?'

And a frown overtakes his face
And I feel a hint of disgrace
That I should try and make haste,
For his face I cannot place,
But from beneath his beard he says,
'It's me.
I used to sit next to you in geography,
And history, and geology.'
'You mean, at school?' I ask.
'No, at the Girl Guides jamboree.
Yes, of course I meant at school,
You freak.
I know it's you, Robert,
I'd recognise those ear lobes anywhere.'

'Toby,' I say, 'how great to see you!
How's it going, dude?
Toby, the Tobe-meister, His Tobeness,

The Tobe-man!
And anyway, what's wrong with my earlobes,
Tobes?'

He says,
'My name's Kevin.
And oh, the years have been so much,
I've really had enough.
I tried so hard to be tough,
But when you reach out for infinity
And dance with sublimity
You kind of forget all the other stuff.

'I've seen moonglow on the Amazon,
The peaks of the Himalayas,
Felt destiny reach in with taloned fingers
And deep down within me, it still lingers.

'I've searched for gold in the outback,
Fished for cod on the Adriatic,
I've run with bandits on the Somalian coast,
And you might think I'm being dramatic,
But I grabbed at life like a thief with a knife,
Made fortune my bedfellow and adventure my wife,
Dancing with the beauty of this planet and its people,
The pulsing rhythm which keeps us all sane.
Life's a game,
And it's all the same,
From the steppes of Russia to the glaciers of Newfoundland.
I even worked a bit as an assistant in Poundland.
I lived my life to the full!'

'So did I,' I reply.
'I've had seven years in finance
And now I'm in logistics.'

He continues,

'Oh, I've had such excitement
And nights of profundity,
Yet in spite of it all
Came the mundanity,
That every profanity
And minor calamity
Only served to undo my humanity,
That the conscience of the majority
Is vile and depraved.
I've seen lesser men pray
That they should be saved,
While wishing that others
Would just go away,
For we are all different,
A species of one,
And though we all live
Under the same blazing sun
There's something inside
Which is constantly undone.

'Through religious oppression
Or the barrel of a gun,
Why learn to love difference
When it's easier to run?
And that's when I decided
To be purposely derided,
To provoke trepidation
And spread consternation
By brandishing broccoli
Outside the station.'

At that moment
I see in him a deeper truth.
'Oh, wise man,' say I,
For my train is due
And I need to pop into Lidl,
'You have altered my way of thinking,

And for the enlightenment I seek,
I shall do the same every week:
Provide sustenance for the meek,
By standing proudly at the airport,
And brandishing a leek.'

And he says,
'That's a bit odd,
Isn't it?'

ON SHIRTLESS ROOFERS

I want to be a roofer.
I want to take my shirt off.
I want to be a slinky roofer
With my shirt off.
I want to look good
With my shirt off.
I want to work on the roof and
Be so slinky that I
Can take my shirt off.
I want to be a roofer.
I want to have astonishing
Stomach muscles
From carrying up and down ladders
Roofing paraphernalia.
I want people to see me from
Passing trains and
Think, *Strewth.*
Look at him on that roof
With his astonishing stomach muscles.
Slate tiles and stinky felt.
And a slinky roofer
With his shirt off.
Just one of the lads,
All hard hats,
Minding his own biz
In his high-vis,
Out with friends for drinky,
Hear those glasses clinky,
But still remaining slinky.

THE BALLAD OF TOM DALEY

I often get mistaken
For Olympic diver Tom Daley.
It keeps happening.
The classically handsome features,
The tanned, toned physique.
That winning smile.
No wonder people get confused.

If I didn't know any better
I'd think I was Tom Daley too.

When he wears his skimpy shorts
And dives into the water
He wins medals, accolades,
Respect and admiration.
Yet when I wear skimpy shorts
And dive into the
Sausage roll display at Tesco,
I get a police caution.
Where's the justice, Mrs Henderson,
Where's the justice?

Tom Daley climbs the ladder.
Tom Daley jumps right off.
Tom Daley dives.
Tom Daley does a somersault.
Tom Daley hits the water.
Tom Daley swims to the side.
Tom Daley climbs out the pool.
Tom Daley expresses the ultimate in human
Perfection you could buy that lad an ice cream
And he'd be ever so grateful sometimes I
Just bang my head against the wall
With all the frustrations built up over
Forty-two hopeless years during which time I
Have not once been nor ever will be
Tom Daley.

I dreamed he came round
For afternoon tea
And we chatted about
Philosophy
And Professor Brian Cox
And how his shows, informative as they are,
Might be half an hour shorter
If he didn't speak
So
Slowly.
The cat wanted to go out and
Tom Daley volunteered.
'Come here, Kevin,' he said.
'Come here.'
The cat's called Kevin.
Sometimes people mistake me for
Professor Brian Cox.

I've started wearing a fake moustache,
Big handlebar moustache,
Handlebar up end curly wax very
Moustachy moustachy
Fake moustache fake moustache
(It didn't cost much dosh),
In case
Someone drops their shopping bag
In the harbour
And some wanker
Suggests I dive in to get it back.

Turned on the TV
To see Tom Daley
Clambering up for another
Dive
And the commentator said,
'Hmmm, that's weird.
Looks like the next competitor
Is Robert Garnham.'

I asked my friend Mark
If I could be as winsome
And as personable
As Tom Daley
And he replied,
'Dear me, no.'

THE OLD LADY WHO SWALLOWED A FLY

There was an old lady who swallowed a fly.
I don't know why she swallowed a fly.
They do odd things at that age.
I don't think she'll die.
She also makes smacking noises with her lips,
But I'm not going to go on about it.
They worry about things, bless 'em.
She swallowed a spider to catch the fly.
It wriggled and tickled and laid eggs inside her.
They had to call an arachnologist.
He found it quite fascinating.
I don't think she'll die.
But she might have psychological trauma.
She swallowed a bird to catch the spider,
Though her stomach acid would most likely have put paid to it.
But it's not worth telling them, they always think they're right.
I don't know why she swallowed a fly,
Though I've seen the way she drinks whiskey, anything's possible.
She swallowed an anteater to catch the bird.
She swallowed the bird to catch the spider
That wriggled and tickled and laid eggs inside her,
And all this after the fly thing that started all this,
And in any case anteaters eat ants, I said to her, Doris,
The clue's in the name.
She swallowed an octopus to catch the anteater.
I said, bloody hell, love, that took some doing.
She said it mostly went down in one lump.

She swallowed the anteater
To catch the bird.
Ironically it actually caught the bird, so
I guess that proves me wrong.
She swallowed a koala to catch the octopus.
I don't know why she swallowed a koala,
Nor do I know where she got one from.
It's a wonder she can afford anything on her pension.
She swallowed the koala to catch the octopus.

She swallowed the octopus to catch the anteater.
She swallowed the anteater to catch the ocelot.
(Sorry, I just realised I missed out the verse about the ocelot.)
She swallowed the ocelot to catch the bird.
She swallowed the bird to catch the spider
That wriggled and tickled and laid eggs inside her.
She swallowed the spider to catch the fly.
I don't know why she swallowed a fly.
I said to her, why did you swallow the fly?
She said, pardon?
I said, why did you swallow the fly?
She said, *Last of the Summer Wine*'s on in a minute.
I said, it's a repeat.
She said, pardon?
I said, it's a repeat.
I don't know why she swallowed a fly.
I don't think she'll die.
I mean,
She will, eventually.

ON BANISTERS

Whenever I go in a building
Which is more than one level
I see banisters.
Banisters next to staircases.
Polished handrail banisters.
Fluted carved wood sectional slats.
Banisters banisters banisters.
They make me angry.

Look at you showing off with your banisters.
You think you're all so high and mighty
Because of your banisters.
If I had banisters I would banish them,
Grind them down, keep them in canisters,
Free from the tyranny of banisters,
Dare I even consider banisters?
Show some sympathy to those
In bungalows
Who have managed perfectly well,
Thank you very much,
Without banisters.
Indoor fence of the soul,
Narrow-columned shield against
Unwarranted ankle glimpse.
Are we really so clumsy on stairs?
Banisters banisters banisters,
Polished banisters,
Varnished banisters,
Painted banisters gloss and emulsion.

People say to me, excuse me,
Where are your banisters?
I haven't got any banisters.
Why haven't you got banisters?
I just haven't got banisters.
What do you do without banisters?
Now listen here, schmuckface, I

Haven't got banisters, I don't like banisters,
I don't want banisters,
Banisters are not for me!

Oh, they really make me angry!
Oh, they stick in my craw!
Oh, they're the height of pretension!

(Fiddly little wooden flourishes
Oh look at me I'm so wonderful
I've got banisters
Tickle little banisters
Tickle little banisters
Go on,
TICKLE MY BANISTERS)

Oh they just stand at the stairs like time softly
Carnivorous waiting
Oh how they love calamity
Oh how I descend into the oblivion of deep and soulless doom
How I rail against thee!

LOCK-IN AT THE LIBRARY

The university library is quiet and still.
Midnight in academia, the doors are locked.
Books softly breathe, relieved
To be alone with their own thoughts.
Except
A professor of literature has got himself locked in.

It's a lock-in at the library!
He skulks along the aisles,
As if lost in the convoluted sentences of
Jorge Luis Borges.
He can't find the door even though
There's a definite door because he thinks
The door is a metaphorical allegory for
The door that divides and yet bonds us
Rather than an actual door
Which is what it is.

He reasons that as this is a library
And he is at the library
He is, therefore, a book,
And then wonders where he'll fit in
Using the Dewey Decimal System.
He tries to squeeze himself between
Botany and Horticulture.

He's intrigued by the wall.
He'd never noticed before that
The library had walls.
He thinks that the boundaries between
Library and non-library have often been
Tenuous at best.
The wall has blown his mind!

And if the library is a library
Then it could easily be a swimming pool.
He tries to swim in a pile of contemporary fiction,

Which backfires when he
Almost drowns in a particularly weighty
Will Self.
We've all been there, professor.
We've all been there.

He thinks he's found his niche.
It's next to the microfiche.

He decides he has to get out
Once he's been scanned at the desk.
He tries to scan himself at the desk.
The scanner doesn't work.
He is not for loan.
He's right at home.
He's all alone.

At least he can wait for the morning
For this torment to end.
But the joke is on him.
It's a bank holiday weekend.

THE PHANTOM MENACE

I've never doubted for a moment
That I'm a stud of the highest order,
A rampant and almost feral specimen
Of rugged masculine sexuality,
And being with you was like
The very definition of bliss,
As heavenly as a unicorn prancing
In a field of daffodils while an
Elf strummed a banjo,
And you can't get much more
Heavenly than that.

But at the height of our passion you shouted out,
'My god,
This is almost as good as
Star Wars Episode I: The Phantom Menace.'

It was a puzzling statement.
Later that night I googled
Star Wars Episode I: The Phantom Menace
And found that, yes,
The anticipation of it had been tremendous,
But it went on a bit
And didn't seem to go anywhere
And the only thing that people remembered
Was the big strange floppy thing
That kind of lolloped around all over the place
With its tongue sticking out.

It didn't even end
With a Big Bang.

I was deeply perplexed
And when I asked you about it,
You said you were
Quoted out of context,
The context being sex,

In which words lose all their meaning,
That anything would have sufficed,
Such as 'Get in,'
'Back of the net,' 'Whammo,'
'He shoots, he scores,'
'Take that, you mega hunk,' or,
As on this occasion,
'This is almost as good as
Star Wars Episode I: The Phantom Menace.'

Perhaps
Everything I knew was wrong.
I watched the film again.
The publicity said it would be a biggy
But it still looked just as stiggy
And Yoda sounded like Miss Piggy.
'Surely,' I said, 'you're a joker.
Am I really so mediocre?'
Yet still you persisted and said
It was an honour to be compared
To *Star Wars Episode I: The Phantom Menace.*

Because that's the kind of man I am,
All show and brash and not much story,
No rebel fighting for some galactic glory
But a jumble of confusion and movement
And noise
And not being able to hear a bloody thing
(No wonder they call it the Deaf Star),
That in a galaxy far far
I should go to some alien gay bar
And end up spending the night
With Jar Jar.

We broke up.
And, bereft, I spent the weeks
In a gloom of my own invention

Until one fantastic night
I found sweet contentment in the form
Of a ruggedly handsome bank clerk
For whom the dance of love was
Conducted with utmost grace
Until, at the heart of our ecstatic passion,
He yelled, 'My god,
This is almost as good as
Star Trek III: The Search for Spock.'

YOU

You.
You struck me with your beauty.
I can never properly describe it.
Not even with the finest thesaurus in the world.
It's so hard.
Difficult.
Problematic.
Troublesome.
Herculean.
The rhyming dictionary didn't help much either.
It gave me a fever.
If only there were some magic lever
To help me get through this,
Become a believer.
Golden retriever.
Telephone receiver.

You.
I'm drunk on you.
You make me woozy.
Last time we met I fell on to the street.
A policeman stopped me,
Said it was because I was staggering.
I said,
'You're not too bad, yourself.'

You.
I cannot disguise my emotions.
I tried.
Went into a joke shop,
Looked for a fake beard.
There were different lengths.
The assistant asked,
'How long do you want it?'
I said,
'Just for the night.'

You.
I think of you when I'm at work,
In the kitchen.
Chopping vegetables with my brother-in-law.
All those hours I've spent
Thinking of you while I'm
Dicing with Geoff.

You.
You drew a fake moustache on my face.
You shaved off one of my eyebrows.
You cracked an egg on my head.
I said,
'You do such strange things to me.'

You.
I keep spending time
Thinking of different parts of you.
A couple of days on your elbows.
Two nights on your left shoulder.
Week at the knees.

You.
Being with you plays with my mind.
I start to question life itself.
What are the chances of slicing bread
And accidentally splitting the atom?
Why do they make the serial numbers
On the sides of reading glasses
So small?
How come the logo for Universal Pictures
Is just of planet Earth?
Why are the three musketeers
Called the three musketeers
When there's four of them
And they don't use muskets?
Life is full of mystery.

You.
You make the world come alive.
The room lights up as you enter
And my heart does that
Tickly little camp little dance it does
When it realises you exist.
You are the you that I would be
If I were you and you were me.
Then you would probably still be you,
So there'd be two of you and none of me
Or maybe there'd be two of me
And I'd be so worried,
Beside myself.

You.
I said to you,
'Will you always be there?'
You said, 'Yes.'
I said,
'Will you always remember me?'
You said, 'Yes.'
I said,
'Will you always, always remember me?'
You said, 'Yes.'
I said,
'Knock knock.'
You said,
'Who's there?'
I said,
'See, you've
Forgotten me already.'

BULK

Out with the lads, Friday night, Jake all lairy and Tom all leery
and all of them pretty beery, darts, pool, lager, perving over
women, playful shoulder punches and heterosexual hugs,
rhythmic belching on a hot summer's night.

And Jake says, 'Here's Pete.'

And, you know, past midnight, the bars still open and the
goodness that dwells within every soul, open-minded and ready
to accommodate this new friend, Pete.

'Alright, Pete?'

Bloody hell!

Pete is a fifty-six-tonne sperm whale.

'Pete's famous,' Jake says, ''cause he can drink like a fish.
Can't you, Pete?'

Pete grins.

His polo shirt only just fits.

'I've just been playing pool,' he says. 'But I leaned on the
table and the legs broke. Completely collapsed! But I won
the game anyway because all of the balls just happened to go
down the holes in the exact right order. We had to leg it.'

I want to ask him how he can leg it when he has not got legs.

'Up till then,' he says, 'it was going swimmingly.'

I also want to ask him how he can hold the cue with his
flappy little fins but I'm afraid he might give me a slapping.

'Let's go out and get a curry,' Jake suggests.

'Or a kebab,' says Tom.

'I don't know about you guys,' says Pete, 'but I'd love some
krill. I think there's an all-night plankton place near here.'

At this moment we hear some loud-mouthed skinhead at the
bar tell a joke in which the punchline denigrates certain sea-
based large mammals.

'Just what did you say?' Pete asks.

The skinhead looks somewhat taken aback.

'Sorry, mate, I didn't realise you were a whale. I couldn't tell
from the accent.'

But now we're beginning to warm to Pete and plans are
made to get a taxi back to our place. Helpfully, Jake suggests
we might need a six-seater, without drawing attention to Pete's

bulk, the elephant in the room.

'We could watch a DVD,' Pete says. 'But not something sad. I always start to blubber.'

'You could stay over,' Tom says. 'I could make up some beds.'

'That's fine, I can always sleep in the bath.'

At that moment a fight breaks out at the pool table. One of the combatants lobs the cue ball; it sails through the air and goes straight into Pete's blowhole, where it lodges, and he dies. The end.

IT'S A SHAME YOU'RE SUCH A SLAPHEAD

It's a shame you're such a slaphead.
It's a shame you've got no hair.
Where once I'd run my fingers through,
Now there's nothing there.

It's a shame you've got no follicles.
It really is obscene.
To get that glow that we both know
You now use Mr Sheen.

The nights we spent together,
The sex on which we'd binge
Now happen so infrequently
They're gone just like your fringe.

You now like Jean-Luc Picard.
You've changed your point of view.
You've started wearing baseball caps.
You have no need of sham
Pooooooooooooooo.

You had such wild and rampant hair
As well as testosterone.
You asked me what the hell I was carrying.
'Honey,' I said, 'it's a comb.'

You call me so very superficial.
Your life is one of hard knocks.
You say I'm so very narrow-minded
'Cause I miss your rampant locks.

It's a shame you're such a slaphead.
You used to be such a tease.
You'd strip off nightly 'cause you were so hot.
Now you're feeling every breeze.

It's a shame you're such slaphead,

But who am I to care?
You're still the same man deep within,
Except you've got no hair.

It's a shame you're such a slaphead.
It's a shame you've got no hair.
Where once I'd run my fingers through,
Now there's nothing there.

KEVIN AND NATALIE

A subtle breath of wind
Lifts net curtains from the frame.
Songbirds pepper the air
With their sweet refrain.
The couple upstairs
Are at it again.

How rampantly sexual, how prolific they are,
How fertile these intrepid lovers,
Kevin and Natalie.
How potent his charms,
How coquettish her laugh.
Kevin has six chins, a beer belly,
And a big drooping moustache.
And so does Natalie.

Syncopated, rhythmic groaning
Provides a slow sensual drumbeat.
I've turned up *Newsnight*
As far as it will go.
Oh, the noise, the grunting,
The big thud as he throws
His grundies to the floor.
I find myself mesmerised;
It's like a never-ending head-on collision
Involving a rhinoceros
And another rhinoceros.

The Jehovah's Witness who called earlier
Told me to listen to the voices from on high.
Today the voices from on high were saying,
'You know you want it, big fella.
Beg me for it.
Go on, beg me for it.'
'Hang on a second, let me
Put down my sausage roll.'

I try to work out the logistics
Of how they do it.
There's got to be some secret method.
It must be like trying to
Find a needle in a haystack,
Only the haystack is wearing a T-shirt
Which reads, 'Official boob inspector
Please form a queue.'

And then they start making noises.
He sounds like a drunken cart horse
Trying to sing 'Minnie the Moocher' at a
Wedding karaoke.
She sounds like a puzzled Neanderthal
Trying to work out how to retune a Freeview box
Because ITV4 has suddenly gone missing.
And when they finally get somewhere
She yells, 'Take me, Des Lynam,
I'm yours!'

You always know it's going well
When he starts whistling.
You always know it's going really well
When she joins in.
Last night must have been excellent
Because they both belted out
The theme tune to *The Wombles*.

Every night I know it's coming.
It's like living in an earthquake zone,
Fearing any moment that this could be
The Big One.
I can hear
Each squirt, squelch, slap and
Fart of their ungainly coupling.
And an odd noise like an elephant with
Trapped wind

Trying to squeeze the last drops
From a washing-up bottle,
Dreading the moment of climax when,
For some reason,
Natalie shouts out every flavour of
Pot Noodle she can think of.

Chow mein. Chow mein.
Chow mein.
Beef. Beef.
Beef.
Oh, CHICKEN AND MUSHROOM!

They're doing it up there.
They're doing it and I'm not.
I'm down here doing nothing
And they're doing it,
As if each whisper, each groan,
Each moment of their bliss
Is but a finger pointed at me
Saying, you have no one,
You have no one,
You. Have. No one.

This sort of thing
Never used to happen
When I lived in a bungalow.

THE WIZARD

I met a wizard, a sage,
A man of his age
Whose wage was to lift
His spells from the page,
Engage with souls and enrage
As if locked in a cage,
Mix emotions, persuade, rampage,
Oh, how I would gauge
With a hint of outrage
As I performed on the stage.
He was an old man
So he wasn't teenage.
His name was Adrian
But his friends called him Adge.

I said,
'Wise man,
Tell me why people are suffering,
For when my heart is fluttering
I hear a low muttering.
It's happening right now
Over the coughing and spluttering,
Like a YouTube clip
That won't stop buffering.

'Why is this world filled with hate and with
Torture, and hunger and greed,
People who don't get what they need?
It's like hatred has planted a seed
Which won't go away
Until we are freed,
Plus a lot of people
Routinely lose their car keys,

'And soldiers,
Dressed in their khakis,
So glib their humour, so sarky,

So cold outside, it really is parky,
It's a lark, see.
Oh, wise man, I beseech thee,
You could teach me,
I'm out of reach, see.
If I was a germ you could bleach me.
Oh, wise man, unleash me.'

He opened his mouth to speak, see,
Thought about it deeply,
Cleared his throat and said,
'Well—'

And I said,
'Give me all your learnings, I'm yearning
To feel that burning
And the world turning,
Life is unfurling,
Like ideas thrown in the air
I'm hurling
Concepts at ya.
What philosophy can we capture,
Or otherwise enrapture?
Tell me, wise man,
Have you got it beat?
Is the street your retreat to make
Your life complete
Like a celebrity retweet?
Tell us why
Life ain't so sweet.'

He pondered and said,
'The trouble is—'

And I said,
'I crave the truth, quell the horror in my brain,
The souls I fear who die in their millions,

The humanity of which we are all a part,
I no more fear the truth, let it blaze like a bonfire
As it wells from deep within, for I cannot help but cry
At all the lies that blind us,'

And he said, 'The thing is—'
And I said,
'Blinded by the claptrap,
I'd rather eat a flapjack,
Drive around in a hatchback,
Wear a backpack,'

And he said, 'If I might interject—'
And I said,
'Back catch,
Sack crack,
Hackensack,
Crackerjack,
Luggage rack,
Quarterback,
Pontiac,
Anorak,
Piggyback,'

And he just walked off.

AIKALOOVIK, ALONE

Metal ice-tiger scratchy comes a frost
Crystal pure and pristine,
Pressing and insistent, almost omniscient,
Parka hood fur imitating short panic draughts,
Gasps, breathe in, breathe out,
Young eyes scanning a blank horizon.
From this rocky shoreline

You can hear the ice floes groan as if giving voice
To the otherwise unspeakable,
A permanent murmur, a whisper,
Oh, brazen child of the north,
Whose urges claim nonexistent victims,
Obvious selfhood, shunned by Inuit elders
Who profess to know more the secrets of
Those creatures that surface occasionally,
Spears thrown, blubber sawn in the freezing salt air,
Than the workings of the human heart.

No myth, no knowledge, no tribal throat songs,
No precedence, no warmth, the sun barely able
To lift its head above a frozen sea which creaks and ripples.
Ice mountains loom and pass so silent after dark,
Ghost ships, lost dreams, phosphorus, a slip of history, a mistake
Of biology in a land of forgetting, and each withered soul
A fortress of freezing; how low can the body's temperature

Fall before a tingle of promise is extinguished or else
Subsumed beneath the tedium of life's great calamities:
Desire, lust, forbidden imaginings, masculine flesh?

078903809041

Don't you worry about me,
I'm really not so lonely,
For I have the perfect plan
To find the perfect man.

There's loneliness in abundance
And gay bars are redundant
And Grindr is such a grind
Though I'm on it all the time.

So weird that I get no action,
Not even the hint of attraction.
And catching the eye of some handsome guy
Makes him quicken his pace. I wonder why.

But feel sorry for me no more,
For written on the door of cubicle number four
In the bogs next to Lidl with the slippery floor,
The kind of phrase that thrills me to the core:

I love fat blokes.
Call this number
For a guaranteed shag.
078903809041.

I'm sure it's not a cruel joke,
But the penmanship of his stroke,
So artistic it's almost baroque,
And, after all, I'm a fat bloke.

And the fact he's done it in permanent ink
Really makes me stop and think
That a life so low could now be at the brink
Of potential orgasm.

The road to contentment is swervy
And I've always been a touch nervy.

The morals are somewhat topsy-turvy.
To be honest it does sound a bit pervy.

I love fat blokes.
Call this number
For a guaranteed shag.
078903809041.

My life should be filled with glee
That this mysterious he
Should live a life so open and free
And to think, I only went in for a wee!

I should treat him just like a brother.
How amazing that I should discover
Someone who would take for his lover
A man with an excess of blubber.

I see it almost as a duty.
I'm not the kind to be snooty.
Chances are he's probably a cutie
Who for some unspecified reason somehow can't get a date
In spite of his stunning handsomeness and sporty physique.

The language he uses to describe
The emotions he'd otherwise hide
Like poetry dancing inside,
Fortune enmeshed with pride.

I love fat blokes.
Call this number
For a guaranteed shag.
078903809041.

I imagine him naked and virile,
The room lit up with his smile
As he says,

'Way hay,
Who ate all the pies?
Let's get down to this, big fella.'

Life can make you feel a chump.
One moment flying, then down with a bump.
I thought I'd get love or someone to hump,
But it was someone mucking round
While they were having a dump.

ECUMENICAL

Waiting at a bus stop,
No idea when the next one was due.
At that moment, a mighty light shone around,
Heavenly choirs singing in all their heraldic majesty
As an angel divine lit by celestial fires
Descended from on high and said,
'Should be one along in about four minutes.'

'Thanks,' I said.
'How ecumenical.'

Just about to bung a ready meal in the microwave.
They make the writing so small on the packaging.
Couldn't find my glasses anywhere.
At that moment, a piercing glow lit up the room,
Heavenly choirs singing in all their heraldic majesty
As an angel holy with passion-imbued fervour
Descended from on high and said,
'Three minutes on full heat, stir, then two and a half,
Then stand for a minute before serving.'

'Thanks,' I said.
'How ecumenical.'

I've been searching for angels
In all the wrong places.
I imagine them vivid,
I think of their faces.

I log on to Gaydar
And see them so sexy,
But they are not angels.
It really does vex me.

They offer no blessings,
Only vague promises.
They send me knob pictures.
It's put me off sausages.

Passion intensity with Aaron from the nightclub.
Losing ourselves to the obvious in my bedroom,
Oh, how feverish our lovemaking, the rhythm
Building up intense as the anticipation
Of solid bliss drove us on to the absolute, oh,
At that moment a piercing light lit the room,
Heavenly choirs singing with all their heraldic majesty
As an angel fervent with omniscient glory
Descended from on high and said,
'Oops, sorry,
I'll be back some other time.'

ZEBRA

You're on, I said,
Once the challenge had been proffered
That I couldn't
Snog a zebra.
You're on,
As I'm feeling particularly perky
And there's something
Spanking about a
Damn good zebra.

Seems everyone's at it, these days.
Zookeepers have put up signs
Warning people off kissing zebras,
At least
Not without first
Practising on a horse.

And that lad in the papers,
Mistook a rhino for a zebra.
Not a very bright lad.
The rhino, having sat on a
Freshly painted white park bench,
Took umbrage.
That's not a zebra,
His friends called,
And he was mauled,
And the rhino never
Answered his texts.

The stripes.
The swishy tail.
The long nose.
Those eyelashes.

To kiss a zebra to kiss a zebra to kiss a zebra
You have to think like a zebra,
So says the Dalai Lama,
But not everything in life is black and white.

I spoke to a zoologist.
He said the worst thing of all
Would be the smell
But the zebra would soon get used to it.

Just close your eyes, he said,
And pretend it's someone else.
C'mon c'mon c'mon,
The first person who springs to mind.
You really have to think on the hoof.

And this fashion
For winding them up!
Making them angry!
On purpose!
Oh, this accursed craze of
Zebra crossing.
Stampeding herds of them In the supermarket
Causing chaos with the
Bar code scanners.
Beep beep beep.
Baked beans, courgettes,
The western suburbs of Bratislava,
Ennui, a duck pond,
The planet Jupiter.
Beep beep beep.
Unexpected item in the bagging area
And zebra droppings near the magazines.

The stripes.
The swishy tail.
The long nose.
Those eyelashes.

I went to the savannah

To look for a zebra
With my friend Joanna
And her sister Deborah
And some lip balm.
I bought some insect repellent.
I bought some breath freshener.
I bought thirty-two tubes of toothpaste.
I bought some evaporated milk but when I opened the tin, it
     was gone.

Jeff asked if he could film it
And put it on a website.
I asked him what kind of website.
He went very quiet.

Noted TV naturalist David Attenborough
Says there's always a chalky aftertaste.

Advancing on the monochrome quadruped,
Advancing through the undergrowth,
Advancing and puckering up,
Come here, my pretty,
Advancing feeling I could just reach out,
Come here, my scrumptious,
Advancing,
That's it, here we go then,
Bending in for a good old-fashioned
Smackeroo.

Well, that was embarrassing.
Last place you'd expect to meet a fan of
Newcastle United.

Close to giving up,
Imagine my luck:
On the flight home
The steward was a zebra

And when I told him of my plight
Halfway through the flight
His eyes lit up with delight.

POEM

You know when the *Titanic*
Finally started to go under?
I was having a dump at the time.
I thought something was amiss
When I pulled the flush
And a squid plopped out.
I shouted to the missus,
'There's a squid in here!'
Then I remembered I wasn't married.

Someone yelled,
'It's time to evacuate!'
I said,
'I just have!'

Oh, Leo, come and save me!
I'd seen him and his girlfriend on the
Front of the ship
Doing that arms-wide thing.
How romantic.
I did the same thing later
With the love of my life
But a seagull swooped down and
Stole my hamburger.

Oily seamen
Down in the boiler room.
Oily seamen
Down in the boiler room.
'Excuse me, lads,
Who do I complain to about
Not getting enough ice
In my martini?'
I enquired
Ironically
Just as we hit the iceberg.

I popped my head in
The control room door.
'Oi, Smiffy,
What the hell was that
All about?'
He said,
'I thought it would swerve first.
I had right of way.
To be honest,
I've had better days.
I'm out of my depth
And it's making me sick.
I suppose I shall have to go
Down with this ship.'
I said,
'Let me know how that turns out.'

'You see,'
An expert in shipping design said,
'Its vast metal hull is
Held together by giant bolts.'
'Wow,' I said,
'That's riveting.'

I saw the chief chef
Punching hell out of a lettuce.
That's why I didn't overly worry
When I'd heard we'd
Struck an iceberg.
Just a glancing blow, Mrs Henderson,
Just a glancing blow.

And the band played on
And on and on.
'A Life on the Ocean Wave'.
Handel's Water Music.
'Hey, kids,

Hey, you kool kats.
Do you know
DJ JD Deejay D and the Funkspewers Collective,
"Dub Fat Da Beat"?

Yo yo dudes,
I ain't got no blues
'Cause it looks like life
Is paying its dues.
It's a big fat beat
And I can't feel no heat.
I'm a fly boss muvva
From my head to my feet.
This is way low.
This is waaaaay low.

Mmm mmm mmm mmm mmm mmm
Mmm mmm mmm mmm mmm mmm.'

They said no,
They hadn't heard of that one.

Bulkheads filling with water.
Compartments filling with water.
Storage decks and engine rooms,
All of them filling with water.
The whole ship started to tilt,
Which completely buggered up
The snooker game I was playing.
'For God's sake,' I said,
'As if the day couldn't get any worse.'
All the balls went in the bottom left.
I knew something was going on
Because my opponent was a narwhal
Using his long nose tusk
As a snooker cue.

POEM

The first time I had a mango
I knew life would be different.
The world seemed a better place.
It was almost as good as
A Chicken McNugget.

Biting into the mango
Made me all queasy inside.
Drooling drip mango juice
Clinging to my chin,
Mango juice
Oozing down,
Dripping on to my chest, all
Matted into my chest hair.
Lick it off, Ben,
Put down that rockhopper penguin and
Lick it off.

(Ben is a marine biologist.)

I don't want to go on
About life before I had the mango.
Back then certain things seemed
Just out of reach,
Like optimism,
Contentment,
And being able to adequately
Describe
Eating a mango.

I went to the greengrocer's.
He said, 'You don't look like
The sort of bloke who eats peaches.'
I said,
'What are you trying to insinuate?'
He said,
'Don't get fruity with me.'

121

I said,
'That's funny because you're a greengrocer
And you said don't get fruity with me.'
He said,
'They're down the back, next to the melons.'

A rare primate was driving his delivery van
While drinking something fizzy from a can.
I said,
'Which way did the mango Tango orang-utan van go?'
He said,
'I've heard about your sort.'

You can fondle them
As much as you like, Mrs Henderson,
But eventually you'll
Have to pop one of them into your gob.
I saw two of them last week
Jumping on the bus.
'What's that all about?' she asked.
I said, 'They've gone off.'

I put a mango into the blender.
I call my blender Glenda.
I put a mango into the blender.
I call my blender Glenda.
I put a mango into the blender,
Juiced it up, mashed it up,
Crushed and stamped and bashed it up,
Then poured it slowly over my head and said to Ben,
'You know what to do, big boy,
You know what to do.'
And he said,
'The man's here to read the meter.'

It's a natural aphrodisiac.
A whole crate of them was

Stolen from Sainsbury's
By hardened criminals.

I made duck à l'orange with mango.
I made chicken tikka with mango.
I made peach melba ice cream
With mango.
And one day for dinner
We just had a mango.
'What's the secret ingredient?' he asked.
It's mango.

It's staring you in the face,
You tosser.

Oooooooo.
Ooooooooooo!
Ooooooooo.
Ooo.
Ooo.
Oooooooo.
Mangos.

Darling, pass me one of those.
I've got the urge.

STEADFAST

Imagine a prison
Impossible to break from
Yet without physical form.
Invisible walls
Built not of brick but of pain,
Notions, expectations,
Life ruined by the abstract.

There are others of your kind,
Unseen in their struggle,
But the very nature of your own
Unique and sublime imprisonment
Blinds you to them.
Rather than fight, they lie
Or else ignore the obvious,
Faces sweating behind bitter masks.

Those who are fortunate
Fill you with anger.
Their love is naught but luck,
And how lucky they love.
Another bead of sweat rolls
Beneath your jaded caricature.
They're so immature!

You dance in your mind,
Rhythms so sensual,
Pounding party silly rhythms,
Inexplicable sun shining smiling
Fresh-faced rhythms incomprehensible
That fact should swamp denial.
Go on, dance, close your eyes and
Dance and let yourself go in a
Way that shouldn't be disco lights
Flashing almost unbelievable as you
Submit to the bounty of freedom
Sugar flip heart thump moving

Fingers across the forbidden and
Not one ounce of tired regret.
Just don't. Open. Your. Eyes.

Steadfast in your culture,
Grey tomb of the senses,
Flesh unblemished to the whip crack,
Absolute devotion to the ether,
Shouting loudest through sheer pride.
You've got to do what's right.
You've got to do what's right.
You've got to do what's right.

Imagine a prison
Impossible to break from,
Not one, but many,
As many prisons as there are poets
And in some places more than others.

FILMSTAR

A stranger afloat on tired Arctic detritus,
Earnest cheekbones too wholesome for a bad climate,
Hair so wild as to detonate the dawn,
He oozes promise.

Any community offers warmth, you feel, and he
No more than the next with his affected youthfulness, healthy
    aura.
When scientists arrive to drill and probe the winter ice
You hightail it, hand gripping the pickup roof strap,

Along ice highways, unmade roads and bitumen,
Tall fir trees and traces of snow slumped slushed,
Cobbling over boulders, townships, remote settlements,
Airstrips where no one guards against inquisitive polar bears.

How tempting does the big city rise from the shale-banked river,
Towering and mighty with its huts and cabins and a main road
So long it twists into the circling woods, this mega metropolis
So big it has its own general store, bar, hospital, car park,

Where your companion bids a fond farewell, cab fan heater
Giddying the moment further than necessary, the city warmth
Hitting you that it might be more than zero degrees, positively
    tropical.
There's an amusing moment where he seriously thinks that you
    think that

This is New York, or Los Angeles, a humorous misunderstanding,
And you think that he thinks that you think he's having you on, and
Then there's this kind of logical dance until you both laugh and he
Welcomes you to the hardy northern township of Caribou Spit.

Wild like a fox in the night near the dream of a soul
By a fire across the valley of passion,
Chilling like a howl from a wolf in the glare of the moon
On the snow by a cabin in the forest of love.

PERMAFROST

All that glitters is not frost.
All that's dreamed will soon be lost.
Cold souls seldom thaw,
Emotional intensity, a pain so raw,
Impossible unions in the late summer sun,
Long dark nights bereft of fun,
What's knotted so tight
Can seldom be undone.
You whisper,
'Soon, the spring will come.'

Sad eyes scan a landscape bereft of love.
It's hard to dance when the rhythms are imposed
From above.
One day, from across the ice, the barren wilderness,
The tundra,
A shout of passion louder than thunder
And chance sublime enmeshed in flames,
But until that time the silence reigns.

BULK CARRIER

Our history books are filled with tales of derring-do,
adventurers, seafarers, salty sea dogs and peg-legged captains,
fishy tough heroes whose brine-soaked beards cling with
moisture like jewelled suspended stars, salt-caked jackets
hardened with oceanic excess. How inspiring their talk of
naughtiness on the high seas, masts aglow with St Elmo's
fire, pirates in the rigging and the infernal discharge of rusty
blunderbusses. Yet things are certainly different these days.

On a millpond sea inky black,
Reflecting stars in all their celestial
Magnificence,
The container vessel MSC *Mercury Thora Hird*,
Hulking, its behemoth hull
Silent as a ghost,
Ploughing between continents with
Crates of tat,
Plastic merchandise, dodgy exports.

Intrepid at heart, though in actuality hired only by the shipping
company to trim the topiary which decorated the atrium of
the main stairwell, Keith Pinkerton found himself, once the
privet had been clipped, with long hours each day in which
there was nothing for him to do. So he would wait for the fall
of night, feeling the ghosts of seafarers past rise up within
him, eschewing the company of his fellow shipmate for solitary
wanderings amid the crates.

He creeps past creaking metal boxes,
Alone,
For it is a sultry night,
The hot metal deck throbbing,
Equatorial,
Towering containers intersecting,
Stacked upwards all angular,
Forming skyscrapers and city blocks,
Grid iron walkways,

An imaginary city
With a population of one.

And the breeze
Which whistles through.

He finds a private place,
A rectangular courtyard of his own
Near the bow, stark,
That he might lie there
Surrounded by right angles
And commune with the sighing wind.

Deep powerful engines
Throb through him,
Pulsing their diesel propulsion
As he stretches out flat on the deck
Coated thick with non-slip paint,
The stars above unmoving,
The universe
So soothing.

From the ether, a miasma, a fog of sudden form, eerie solidity
within the sea spray taking the shape of a man with an
exuberant moustache. Whoever could this half-formed phantom
be? A pirate from days of yore, a sailor with malevolent intent, a
sea devil in human form, about to take his soul?

Or is it the ghost of early twentieth-century French novelist
Marcel Proust, for some reason?

'Bonjour,' he says.
So possibly the latter.
'What do you want from me?' Keith asks,
Taken aback by the sudden apparition and, bizarrely,
Checking to see if his flies are undone.
'I've been watching you,' says Marcel Proust.

'Whatever for?'

'The sea is filled with macho types, hurly burly heroes and sailors with ripping biceps, rugged battleship commanders and submariners; there's nothing out here for a man like me except about once every now and then when a cruise ship comes through with an ABBA tribute band. How lifeless, how barren this place can be, for someone like me.'

The sea heaves like a breath exhaled.
Containers groan with obviousness.
Stars in all their beautiful magnificence,
Omniscient.

'Am I really so camp?' asks Keith.
'Oh, please,' Marcel replies, 'you're camper than a bus full of
    mermaids being driven by a starfish.'
'I thought I hid it well,' Keith replies.
'You're lucky,' says Proust.
'I come from a time where the love I had
Could never be revealed, only hinted at.
But I had a cunning plan, subtly changing the names of the men
I adored in my fiction
And giving them feminine approximations.
Albertine. Josephine. Geraldine. Henrietta.
Roberta.
Nobody suspected a thing!'

'What do you want from me?' Keith asks.

'The first time I saw you,
Off the coast of Cameroon,
Lit by the moon,
Down in the boiler room,
My heart went boom.
Titty boom.
Titty boom.'

But Keith is not impressed.
'You don't know what my life is like,' he says.
'Nights in lonely cabins.
My formative years at naval college,
The whole time
Gazing at my belly button.
Then an apprenticeship
On a battleship
Learning the ropes
On the HMS *Hindrance*,
Lonely bunks and
Shirtless hunks,
Dockside manners and
Gangplank dreams,
A life surrounded
By seamen.'

'Dance with me,' says Marcel.
'Dance with me
To the music of movement.
We all carry baggage
And various cargoes.
Dance with me
To the memory.
I'm serious,
Delirious.
Dance with me
In the midnight burn.
This may be the bow
Of the ship
But I'm really
Quite stern.
Dance with me.'

'Not right now,' says Keith.

He asks Marcel if Marcel loves him and Marcel says that he

most certainly does and he tells Marcel that he really will have to stop this nonsense and Marcel replies, 'Every relief is just the postponement of grief, Keith,' and Keith says, 'What does that mean?' and Marcel says that his life is already incredibly complicated what with the fact that he lives on a container vessel and it has lots of stress what with looking after the topiary in the main atrium and that if the captain should one day see even the smallest speck of aphids or greenfly then he might go off on one, and Marcel says, 'Let me comfort you,' and Keith says no, no, no, and Marcel tells Keith that it really is like they're from two different worlds, and then he evaporates into a cloud of sea spray.

The tinny tap of workboot on the moving metal floor speckled damp by sea spray and hardened salt in this dank deck quick step so very much like falling through someone else's dreamscape look at him now he's got the rhythm baby he's got the moves not like last week when he threw his back out while dancing to Kylie in his cabin oh how he's put everything into this ship, every emotion and every aspect of his being, oh, the hull is the sum of its parts.

He winds his way back towards the accommodation deck,
Back through the darkened blocks.
The tall gleaming bridge,
Letting himself back in to its
Industrial brightness.

At that moment a shimmering brightness, a kaleidoscopic
    coalescence of
Mist and sea fog taking on the most ludicrous shape, and from
    nowhere,
From the ether, appears the unmistakable flamboyance of
    Oscar Wilde.

'Dearest Keith!' says he,
To which Keith replies,

'Yeah, not right now, thanks,
I've had a rough night.'

And he goes back to his bunk and
Furiously masturbates while
Thinking about Justin Bieber.

The next morning the ship sinks, the end.

LOADING THE DISHWASHER WITH MONTSERRAT CABALLÉ

Part One

That fork goes in the cutlery receptacle,
And the spatula too.
And the egg whisk and the cake dishes
And the garlic press.
A special compartment for utensils;
That includes the spatula.
I love you.

Dance with me in the splendour of it.
Polished metal sheen fantastic machine.
I adore you, Montserrat Caballé.
Soft hands as we fumble briefly
Over the crock pot,
Soft hands caressing soapy suddy crock pot,
Rampant urges over the kitchen sink,
Dishwasher door mouth agape like a basking shark.

You tried my mother's homemade hot pot,
Ate the lot
Wiped your sweating brow with a serviette.
My friends all think I'm pervy, yet
I'm not.
Some of them call me a crackpot,
But when you tucked into that hot pot
I knew I'd hit the jackpot.

Some of it is still round your mouth, Montserrat Caballé.

Part Two

Here it comes now
Grumble grumble
Lights aflicker

Clonking clicking
Churning churning
Water filling
Pipes agurgle
Cogitating
Thanks for waiting
Sort of gurgling
Is it working?
Grumble grumble
Here it comes now
Speeding up now
Soft vibrations
Ruminations
Hesitations
Here it comes now
One two three four
Here it comes now
Here it comes now

Cashonga-clunk
Cashonga-clunk
Cashonga-clunk
Cashonga-clunk
Cashonga-clunk
Cashonga-clunk

Part Three

What is it that you want?
– Did you put the teapot in?
Yes, I put the teapot in.
– Did you put the saucepan in?
Yes, I put the saucepan in.
– What about the saucepan lid?
We never used the saucepan lid.
– Yes we did.

No we didn't.
– Yes we did.
No we didn't.
– Yes we diiiiid.

We didn't use the saucepan lid.
We simmered gently, yes we did.
We drained the water with a plate.
The steam rose up, it felt so great.
We didn't use the saucepan top.
That is why I shouted, 'Stop!
Put it back where it should go.'
You asked me why and I said no,
The saucepan lid we did not use.
That is why I get the blues.
You bully me because you can,
You never let me be a man,
And I feel so belittled now
Because we've had this stupid row.
We didn't use the saucepan lid.
We didn't use the saucepan lid.
We didn't use the saucepan lid.
We didn't use the saucepan lid.
Come to think of it, we did.

I'm sorry that I hurt you.
Didn't mean to make you cry.
I'm sorry that I hurt you.
At least the dishes all are dry.

Part Four

Utensils aplenty!
Oh, how you love utensils.
It might all end tomorrow
Halfway through making a meringue.

You'd leave me, taking all your utensils.
But that's just a whisk you've got to take.

I can't remember which day
I drained some pasta.
Monday, Tuesday or Wednesday.
I'll have to check it on the colander.

Oh, how jealous you are of
My apple corer.
Mind you, it is appealing.

The thing with the jagged holes
Or the thing with the serrated holes.
I can't tell which is the grater.

Part Five

Your tremulous warbling
Echoes back from the dishwasher
Like the call of the blue whale
Intercepted by a marine research vessel.
Your vocal strains carry with them
A plaintive primal aspect
As if giving voice to the fate of
Human existence and that which motivates us
Through life, though it doesn't stop
The neighbours banging on the walls;
Downton Abbey is on.

I have a tea towel pleasantly folded
And ironed with freshness brightness clean:
An invitation, which, sadly,
You completely ignore.
As I open the door, steam rises,
Glistening from the stippling on the ceiling

Like gravity-defying mountain dew inverted.
You stand in my kitchen like a phantom in the mist
Hovering ever so gently, knowing that at
Any moment I might ask you to help unload.

Unload.
Unload the pots.
Unload the plates, unload the
Cups and the mugs and the beakers and the knives
And the ladles and the masher and the butter dish,
Unload the whole blooming lot in all of your saintly glory,
You absolute heart-thumping ever so subtly hubba-bubba
Soft-skinned lightly perfumed nymph-like splendour,
Unload the lot and place it in the cupboards like it
Means so much more than a domestic chore, the
Two of us opening cupboard doors and kitchen drawers,
Laughing and exchanging glances before we lose
Ourselves to the passion which lingers deep inside and
The dishwasher stands empty, ready to fight another day!

But instead you say,
I'm going home.
I'm going home.

THANKS TO

I tried to write a 'thanks to' list, but it was about three pages long. Nobody wants to read that. And then I kept remembering people I'd forgotten. And then I started thanking people like the man in the newsagent's and the lady on reception at the leisure centre. And then Melanie Branton said that everyone who gets thanked should automatically get a free copy of the book. By this time I had 113 people on the list and I was still going strong. That would have bankrupted me. Not only that, but a lot of people had been saying things like, 'Make sure you list me in the thank-you section of your next book,' which was nice because it showed they were assuming I'd have another book in me. But perhaps they were just after a free copy.

I mean, I suppose I could just generalise and say, 'Thanks to everyone who's been there along the way.' That makes me sound cheap, though, don't you think? So then I thought, why don't I write nothing at all? Because I swear, I never read the thank-you section of a book. What was embarrassing, once, was when someone thanked me in the thank-you section of their book and never told me (and, come to think of it, they even gave me a free copy of the book, so perhaps Mels was on to something), and they hinted, like, 'What did you think of the book?' and I said, 'Yeah, excellent poetry, fantastic stuff,' and they replied, 'It was a book of essays,' and I'm like, 'Oh, it was so wonderfully written and so beautifully evocative that it was just like poetry,' and then two years later I find out that they'd put me in the thank-you section of their book, and I wanted to say to them, 'Thanks for mentioning me in the thank-you section of your book,' but by then we'd fallen out, and they never told me what it was that we'd fallen out over.